Short i and Long i
Play
a Game

written by Jane Belk Moncure
illustrated by Helen Endres

THE CHILD'S WORLD

Library of Congress Cataloging in Publication Data

Moncure, Jane Belk.
    Short "i" and Long "i" play a game.

    (Play with vowel sounds)
    SUMMARY: Introduces the long and short "i" sounds.
    1. English language—Vowels—Juvenile literature.
[1. English language—Vowels]   I. Endres, Helen.
II. Title.   III. Series.
PE1157.M63   428'.1   79-10303
ISBN 0-89565-091-6

Short i and Long i

Play
a Game

This is  . She has a special sound.

Igloo   begins with her

Short "i" sound.

So does Indian.

Indian

igloo

7

This is Long i. He has a different sound.

Ice begins with his Long "i" sound.

So does icicle.

Can you hear the short i and the long i sounds?

Indian

igloo

One day, said, "Let's play a game.
I will look for my sound in words.

icicle

ice

And you can look for your sound in words.
We'll see who can find the most words."

 found inchworms,

many, many inchworms.

Then she found iguanas,
many, many iguanas.

"I will win!" she said.

found an iris

and an island.

He also found an   iceberg.

"No!   I will win!" he said.

iris

iceberg

icicle

island

ice

Then  counted. "I win," said Long i.
"I have the most words."

inchworms

iguanas

igloo

Indian

 counted. "No! No! No!" she said.

"I will use my eyes

 and ears.

My sound hides in words. I will find words with my sound in the middle of them."

I found a pig

and a fish.

Then she found a ship

and a hippo.

"Now I win!" said Short i.

"No! No! No!" said . "I will use my eyes

 and my ears.

My sound hides in words too. I will find words with my sound in the middle of them."

found a kite

and a bike.

Then he found a pipe,

a dime

and a dinosaur.

"My! My!"
said . "I will surely win!"

fish

Indian

iguanas

pig

inchworms

igloo

ship

hippo

Can you tell

26

kite

iceberg

dinosaur

island

dime

pipe

bike

icicle

ice

iris

Long
i

who won?

Can you read these words with  ?

kitten

ring

swing

brick

king

hill

slipper

witch

Can you read these words with  ?

smile

pie

lion

iron

ivy

tie

hive

spider

Now, you make up a game!